LEARNING RESOURCES CENTER
UNIVERSITY OF WYOMING LIBRARIES
LARAMIE, WY 82071

PAST AND PRESENT
TERRORISM
PHILIP STEELE

New Discovery Books
NEW YORK

Copyright © 1992 Heinemann Educational Books Ltd, 1992

All rights reserved. No part of this book may be reproduced or transmitted in any form or by any means, electronic or mechanical, including photocopying, recording, or by any information storage and retrieval system, without permission in writing from the publisher.

First American publication 1992 by New Discovery Books,
Macmillan Publishing Company, 866 Third Avenue, New York, NY 10022.

Macmillan Publishing Company is part of the Maxwell Communication Group of Companies.

First published in 1992 by Heinemann Children's Reference,
a division of Heinemann Educational Books Ltd., Halley Court,
Jordan Hill, Oxford OX2 8EJ.

Devised and produced by Zoe Books Limited
15 Worthy Lane, Winchester, SO23 7AB, England

Edited by Charlotte Rolfe
Picture research by Faith Perkins
Designed by Julian Holland

Printed in Hong Kong

Library of Congress Cataloging-in-Publication Data

Steele, Philip
    Terrorism / Philip Steele.
      p. cm. — (Past and present)
      Summary: Defines terrorism and chronicles the history of this phenomenon and its increase in recent years.
      ISBN 0-02-735401-6
      1. Terrorism—History—Juvenile literature. [1. Terrorism.]
    I. Title. II. Series: Past and present
    HV6431.S728   1992
    303.6'25—dc20   91-39803
                                                                                                             AC

Photographic acknowledgments

The author and publishers wish to acknowledge with thanks, the following photographic sources:
Camera Press pp 25; 34: Hulton-Deutsch Collection pp 9; 12; 14; 16; 33; 40: Popperfoto pp 4; 42: Rex Features p 6; 19; 22; 26; 29; 31; 37; 39; 43:

The cover photograph is courtesy of Magnum/Marlow

The publishers have made every effort to trace the copyright holders, but if they have inadvertently overlooked any, they will be pleased to make the necessary arrangement at the first opportunity.

The author and publishers are grateful for permission to reproduce a short extract from *The Demon Lover: on the sexuality of terrorism* by Robin Morgan, published by Methuen 1989.

Title page: **Terror on the streets, as a car bomb explodes in West Beirut, Lebanon, in 1985.**

CONTENTS

What is terrorism?	4
The first terrorists	9
The violent century	16
Tactics, weapons, & victims	26
State terror	31
The fight against terrorism	37
Questions of right and wrong	40
Key dates	45
Glossary	46
Index	48

PAST AND PRESENT

WHAT IS TERRORISM?

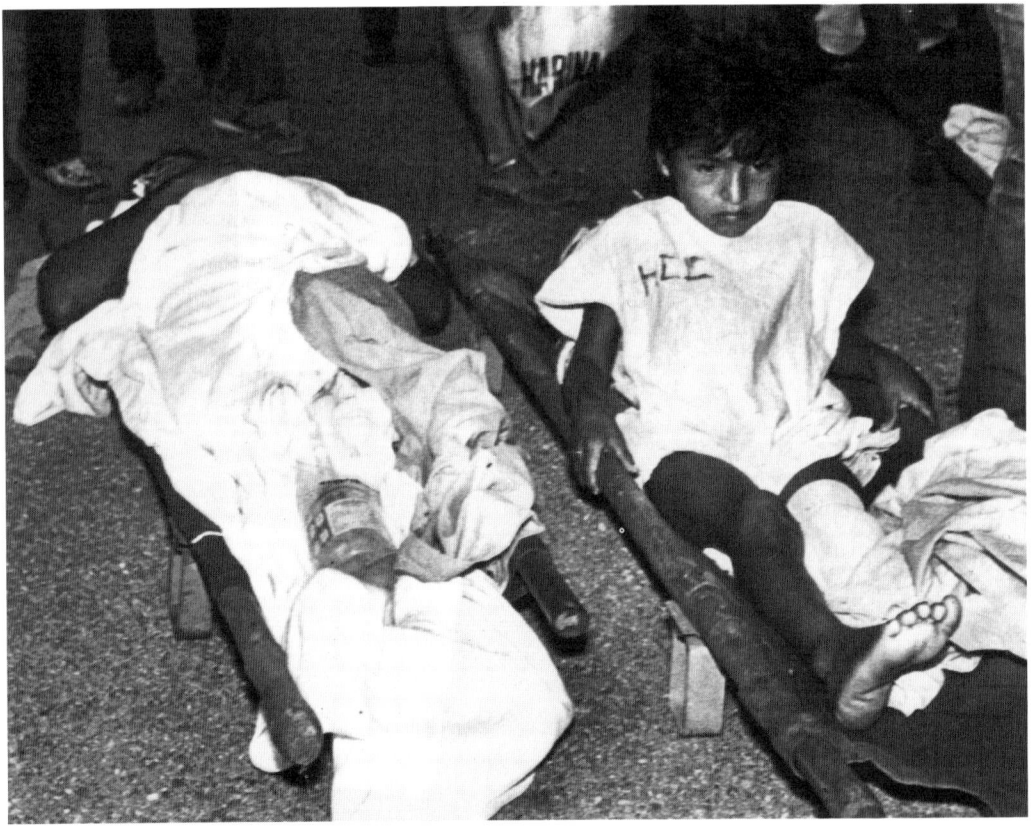

During 1987, 6,000 civilians were killed in Nicaragua by an organization called the Contras. A further 6,000 were injured. This little boy had his foot blown off. The Nicaraguan government accused the Contras of "terrorism." The American president, Ronald Reagan, claimed that the Contras were "freedom fighters."

WHAT IS TERRORISM?

Terrorism is in the news. Bombs explode in public places, killing innocent people. Aircraft are blown up in midair. In just one year, 1989, about 400 terrorist attacks took place around the world, with the loss of about 300 lives. Many other victims were taken prisoner or tortured. Buildings and other properties were destroyed.

One February morning in 1991, mortars were fired from a van parked in Whitehall, in the heart of London. The missiles landed at the back of Number 10 Downing Street, where the British prime minister, John Major, was at a meeting with other government ministers. None of the politicians was injured, but explosions rocked the building. The van burst into flames and its drivers made their escape. The Irish Republican Army (IRA) later announced that they had planned and carried out the attack.

Since the 1970s there has been a big increase in violence of this kind. Modern automatic weapons and electronic devices have made it easier for individuals to cause widespread destruction. Many people have become afraid of international travel, particularly during times of crisis. Airports may be surrounded by soldiers and tanks. Railroad stations may be closed while the police search for bombs.

The chances of being killed by a terrorist attack are small. In wartime, on the other hand, a single night's bombing by a modern air force can destroy the lives of thousands of civilians. But because terrorists seem to be able to strike anywhere, without warning—and sometimes apparently without reason either—they can create a general feeling of uncertainty and fear among the population. When this happens, the terrorists are succeeding in their aims.

NAMES AND CLAIMS

Dictionaries usually explain terrorism as the use of violence for political aims. During the ten years between 1980 and 1990 over 1,000 political organizations claimed responsibility for terrorist attacks around the world. But who are the "terrorists" really?

PAST AND PRESENT

A wanted notice is posted on the streets of Paris. It shows Lebanese men and women wanted in connection with terrorist acts. It warns the public to beware of them, as they may be armed. As you can see, they look like any other young people. If they did become involved in violent attacks, how did this happen? What led them to such drastic action?

Those who wish to hold on to power at any price may use terrorism to control others. For example, governments that rule by fear may capture, imprison, torture, and murder their own citizens. They may use the police or army to terrorize the public. This is called **state terrorism**.

Individual terrorist organizations, on the other hand, may attack members of a government or ordinary people. Their aim is to interrupt everyday life and bring confusion to the normal running of a country. They use violence, or the threat of violence, to press for their own demands.

The violence labeled as terrorist is usually sudden, unexpected, and extreme. It often threatens innocent people. In 1989 it was estimated that nearly half of all attacks by terrorist organizations involved bombing or arson, the burning of property. In over 35 percent of the attacks, weapons were used. The United States Congress has described terrorist attacks as including:
- acts of **sabotage**, such as destroying important buildings or supply lines,
- **hijacking** goods or vehicles,
- taking people **hostage**.

Other types of terrorist activity might include death threats to individuals and the poisoning of food or public water supplies.

The United Nations (UN) was founded in 1945. Its main aim was to secure world peace. The UN now has 166 member states. Many of these have spoken out against terrorist violence, but in spite of the general disapproval, the UN's General Assembly has been unable to find a definition of the word "terrorism" that is acceptable to all its members.

The problem is that people take sides. They may agree with the aims and methods of a particular group — if so, they use words like "freedom fighters" and "armed struggle" to describe the group and its activities. But if they disagree with the group, they use the words "terrorist" and "terrorism." So the word "terrorism" is very often used to criticize and condemn a particular group and its struggle.

Public opinion also changes over time. Some fighters have been criticized by their opponents as "terrorists" during an armed struggle for power. Later they have become widely respected leaders of their country. The UN itself opposes terrorist acts, but it does not condemn those who do these things in the struggle for self-rule, independence, or freedom from racist, colonial, or foreign rule.

> The successful revolutionary is a statesman, the unsuccessful one is a criminal.
>
> *Erich Fromm, psychologist and philosopher (1941)*

WHO USES TERROR?

Many of the methods used by the political terrorist are similar to those used in the criminal world. Criminal organizations such as the Mafia may use terror to control a business or a particular part of a city, but they are not described as terrorists, because their aim is to live off society as it is, not to change things.

Most regular, or national, armies also use violence in order to create terror among the enemy. They often kill innocent civilians during wars, and their special units are trained to kill by stealth. However, few people refer to such attacks as "terrorist." Many people regard the violence used by an army as lawful if the army follows the rules of the Geneva convention. This is an international agreement that says how prisoners and wounded enemy soldiers should be treated.

Guerrillas are groups of soldiers who fight against a regular army or government. Their enemies often refer to them as "terrorists," but they consider themselves to be freedom fighters. Many people who use terrorist tactics like to call themselves guerrillas. Once they are put into action, the actual methods of regular soldiers, guerrillas, and terrorists may be very similar.

THE FIRST TERRORISTS

Throughout the ages, terror has been used as a weapon against people. This man was burned at the stake in sixteenth-century England, simply because of his religious beliefs.

THE ANCIENT WORLD

The histories of ancient Egypt, Greece, and Rome include long lists of political murders, poisonings, and stabbings. Few people protested about these crimes. It was generally understood that those who wanted power would seize it violently. Violence was often seen as the only way to right a wrong.

Those who had positions of power made sure that they were praised by the writers and poets of the day. Their use of terror and violence went down in history as acts of heroism. Those who failed in their attempts to gain power were described as evil. Even before there were newspapers and news broadcasts, facts were covered up or changed for political reasons. Today, we call this **propaganda**.

One of the most famous political murders was that of Julius Caesar in 44 B.C. A group of 60 Roman politicians planned the death of Caesar, who was then the most powerful man in the Western world. They claimed that he wanted to make himself absolute king. Caesar was attacked by a group of senators, and bled to death with 23 stab wounds in his body. However, this act of terror failed to win public support for the murderers or for their cause.

In the ancient Roman empire there were also some terrorist groups that operated in a way familiar to us today. The *Sicarii* ("dagger men") were active between A.D. 66 and 73 in the province of Judaea. At this time there was an uprising of Jews against the Roman forces of occupation in Judaea. The *Sicarii* were an extremist Jewish group who murdered their opponents, often in public places. They sabotaged the water supply and burned down the grain supplies in order to cause confusion and disrupt everyday life. The historian Josephus (A.D. 37 – c.95) described them as common criminals.

HOLY TERROR

The word **assassin** means anyone who murders for a reward or for fanatical or for extreme beliefs. The word comes from the Arabic *hashshashin* ("those who take the drug hashish"). The *hashshashin* were a group of Ismaili Muslims based in Persia (Iran) and Syria between about

1090 and 1272. Their first leader was called Hassan-i-Sabbah. He and his successors, sometimes known as "Sheikhs of the Jebel" or "The Old Men of the Mountains," became feared through much of Asia and Europe. They believed it was their god-given duty to get rid of people who did not share their beliefs.

The *hashshashin* were famed for clever disguises and for surprise attacks. Nobody knew where they would strike next. They believed that when they died they were sure to win a place in paradise, so they showed no fear. Their victims included both Christians and members of rival Muslim religious groups. They killed many important rulers of the day, including Conrad of Montferrat, the Christian king of Jerusalem, who was stabbed to death in 1192.

The Christian church also used terror to defeat its opponents. Members of Christian groups that challenged traditional beliefs were accused of witchcraft and **heresy,** or false beliefs. In 1478 Pope Sixtus IV authorized a team of investigators in Spain, whose job was to seek out heretics and punish them. Many Muslims and Jews who had converted to Christianity were tortured and killed by the "Spanish Inquisition" as it became known, and many political enemies of the Spanish royal family were also falsely accused. Large crowds watched victims of the Inquisition being burned at the stake. The name of the first Inquisitor-General, a monk called Tomás de Torquemada, was feared far and wide.

IN THE SHADOW OF THE GUILLOTINE

The word "terrorism" was first used in France, where it appears in a dictionary of 1798. It originally referred to state terrorism, the action of a government against its own citizens. The French Revolution had begun in 1789 as a people's uprising against poverty and starvation. The French king, Louis XVI, was quickly overthrown, and many people died violently on the streets of Paris. In 1793–1794 some of the revolutionaries who now formed the government, including Maximilien Robespierre, started a "Reign of Terror." During this period over

The guillotine claims another victim, as the figure of Liberty looks on. The piles of heads show the victims of the French state's Reign of Terror in 1793 – 1794. They include clergy, nobles, politicians, and lawyers. The largest pile belongs to those whom the revolution claimed to defend — the people themselves.

300,000 people were arrested, and many of these died in prison without ever coming to trial. About 17,000 were executed. The king himself was sent to the guillotine, and his severed head was displayed to the jeering crowds.

Robespierre and some of his supporters used the word "terror" with approval. They believed that by creating public fear they would protect the revolutionary government. No one would dare oppose them. In the end though, people became sickened by the bloodshed and no longer supported Robespierre. In 1794 he was thrown out of government, arrested and executed. The word "terrorist" became an insult.

THE WILL OF THE PEOPLE
The ideas which originally inspired the French Revolution of 1789 had a great effect on the rest of Europe. People demanded an end to poverty and injustice. In nineteenth-century Europe, many people in the countryside were still living in very poor conditions. Others now worked in factories for low wages and lived in overcrowded and unhealthy housing in the growing cities. Many people wanted to change society. They turned to new political theories, such as **communism** or **anarchism**. These ideas demanded more power for the people, and a greater share in the riches of the country.

Many people rejected violence. Others believed that there was only one way to bring about change and improvement, if individual rulers and governors would not listen. They must use terrorist tactics themselves. In 1872 a group of men and women calling themselves *Narodnaya Volya* ("People's Will") killed the ruler of Russia, Tsar Alexander II. Many revolutionaries in Europe and America decided to follow this example.

> All that is false must be destroyed, without exception and without pity, so that the truth may triumph.
>
> *Mikhail Bakunin,
> Russian anarchist (1814-1876)*

PAST AND PRESENT

Toward the end of the nineteenth century, terrorist attacks became more and more common. In 1886 a bottle of acid was thrown into the Paris stock exchange. In the same year a bomb killed a policeman in Chicago's Haymarket Square and unrest that had started as a workers' protest demonstration turned into a riot. In 1892 a French anarchist called François Königstein, or "Ravachol," set off bombs in public places in Paris and caused widespread panic. An anarchist song of the time included the words *"Vive le son/De l'explosion!"* ("Long live the sound of the explosion!")

On July 29, 1900, King Umberto I of Italy was assassinated by an anarchist while riding in a carriage through the streets of Monza. Some anarchists believed that individual acts of terror were preferable to mass uprisings because fewer people were killed.

One attack followed another. In November 1893 a theater in Barcelona, Spain, was bombed by anarchists and 20 people were killed. In the following month a nail bomb was thrown into the Chamber of Deputies in Paris, France.

As well as attacks on the public, there was a terrorist campaign directed at the world's most powerful rulers. President Sadi-Carnot of France was assassinated in 1894, Empress Elisabeth of Austria in 1898, King Umberto of Italy in 1900, President McKinley of the United States in 1901. McKinley's assassin, an anarchist named Leon Czolgocz, said "I killed the president because he was the enemy of . . . good working people."

These acts of violence succeeded in creating a climate of fear. Popular magazines often included drawings of the "typical" anarchist — a sinister figure in a black cloak, carrying a smoking bomb. Governments and police reacted violently when their turn came. Many innocent anarchists were arrested as terrorists. Of those tried for the Chicago bombing, four were executed, three were imprisoned, and one committed suicide. They were later declared innocent, and the governor of Illinois confirmed that their trial had been unjust.

PAST AND PRESENT

THE VIOLENT CENTURY

A Jewish man is paraded before Nazi bullies. The Nazis were terrorists in uniform who seized power in Germany during the 1930s.

When the New Year arrived in 1900, many people welcomed the new century. They looked forward to a period of peaceful progress. In fact it soon proved to be a century of war, mass murder, and terrorism.

WARS AND REVOLUTIONS

In 1914 the Archduke Franz Ferdinand, heir to the throne of Austria-Hungary, was visiting the town of Sarajevo (now in Yugoslavia). He was unaware that the crowds concealed an assassin, a young student called Gavrilo Princip, who stepped forward and shot and killed the archduke and his wife.

The murder of the archduke shook the world. It had been planned by Serbian nationalists belonging to a terrorist organization called the "Union of Death," or the "Black Hand." "My flaming body will be a torch to light other people on their path to freedom" were Princip's fine words. In fact his deadly attack led millions to their death, for as a result of this assassination, Austria and Germany were soon engaged in a terrible war with France, Britain, and Russia.

Before World War I was over, the Russian tsar Nicholas II had been swept from power by a Communist revolution. Germany and its allies finally surrendered in 1918. Germany was broken in defeat — and provided a breeding ground for a new kind of terrorism.

The National Socialist ("Nazi") German Workers' party was founded in 1920. Its members were violently **racist** and anticommunist. They beat up people on the street, murdered their opponents, and smashed the windows of Jewish shops. They even assassinated their own members as they scrambled for power. The Nazis created a climate of terror in which they finally seized control of the government. They then began one of the most violent periods of state terrorism known in history.

During World War II, from 1940 to 1944, France was occupied by Nazi soldiers. Many French men and women fought against them. They sabotaged factories, blew up railroad lines, and killed their enemies. The Germans viewed them as terrorists, but to the rest of Europe they were resistance fighters and heroes, because they were fighting the Nazis.

FREEDOM FROM FOREIGN RULE

Throughout the nineteenth century, the leading nations in Europe had been increasing their power and wealth. They had founded **colonies** by occupying and governing large parts of Africa and Asia. By the end of World War II, though, the colonial powers in Europe were weakened, and the people in the colonies intensified their struggle for independence and freedom from foreign rule.

The British fought colonial wars in Africa and Asia, and so did the French. One of the many guerrilla groups that fought the European powers was the Algerian *Front de Libération National* (FLN). It was founded in 1954. It fought against the French army throughout the colony of Algeria and also carried out terrorist attacks against the French colonists in the cities. **Urban guerrillas** were hard to track down in the crowded streets and alleys. The FLN was successful because most people supported it. Although it had only 15,000 fighters in the field, it fought effectively against a French army that was over ten times that size.

The French colonists in Algeria also set up their own terrorist organization in 1962, the *Organisation de l'Armée Secrète* (OAS), that tried to prevent the French government from granting independence to Algeria. The OAS murdered their opponents and blew up buildings in France. These terrorist acts did not help them. They only speeded up the French government's desire to make peace with the FLN. Algeria finally won its independence with a huge "yes" vote in 1962.

FRAGMENTED NATIONS

When people in one part of a country wish to break away from it, they are called separatists. Separatist movements have become common in many parts of the world. During the 1960s, Scottish and Welsh nationalists demanded independence from the United Kingdom. Similar demands were made by Basques in Spain, and French-

THE VIOLENT CENTURY

Troops loyal to France rounded up FLN members in Algeria during the 1950s. The FLN was fighting for independence. Both sides used terror as a weapon.

speaking Canadians in Québec. In northeast Africa, Eritreans have been fighting to return to the independence they once had within Ethiopia. Amid terrible violence in Sri Lanka, Tamils have demanded self-rule. Tactics used by many separatist groups have included kidnapping, arson, murder, and robbery. During the 1960s and 1970s the Basque group *Euzkadi ta Askatasuna* (ETA) attacked police and judges and placed bombs in public places, including beaches used by tourists.

Sometimes people who live in one country wish to join another one. In the 1950s many Greeks living on the island of Cyprus joined an organization called *Ethniki Organosis Kyprion Agoniston* (EOKA). They wanted Cyprus to become a part of Greece. They used terrorist tactics to fight the British troops occupying the island. Later the EOKA leader, George Grivas, wrote that the methods of his fighters weren't very different from those of the British commandos.

FIGHTING FOR A NEW SOCIETY
Not all twentieth-century terrorists have been concerned with national borders or independence. From the late 1960s onward there was a return to political terrorism.

As in nineteenth-century Russia, many of the new organizations using terrorist tactics recruited their members from colleges and universities. The students had turned to extreme political actions not because of poverty, but because of bitterness and frustration with a society that they felt was corrupt.

In Germany, the Baader-Meinhof group, part of the "Red Army Faction" engaged in robbery, kidnapping, and murder during the 1970s. They believed that they were fighting the ruling class on behalf of the working class, which had become powerless. They hoped that acts of terror would break down the society they thought was unjust, and create the right circumstances for complete change or revolution. However, they lacked the popular support they needed to succeed.

Similar groups operated elsewhere. In Italy the "Red Brigades" kidnapped and murdered former government leader Aldo Moro. The "Weathermen" operated in the United States, the "Angry Brigade" in England, the "Red Army" (*Sekigun*) in Japan, and *"Action Directe"* in France.

Other terrorist groups were **neofascist.** They wished to re-create the years of terror when the Nazis and **Fascists** seized power. One of the worst terrorist attacks of modern times occurred in August 1980 in Italy, when neofascists planted a bomb at the Bologna railroad station. The bomb killed 79 people and wounded 188. Today flowers are still placed outside the station on a memorial to the dead. Terrorism has claimed over 1,200 victims in Italy alone since 1969.

In the headlines 1: The Irish question

Some political problems have caused fighting and violence for hundreds of years. British rule in Ireland has been bitterly opposed for centuries. What is the story behind the guerrilla warfare and terrorism that we read about today?

During the Middle Ages, English rule covered a small area around Dublin, called "the Pale." Later, English rulers tried to control the whole of Ireland and make it Protestant rather than Roman Catholic. They seized Irish lands and gave them to their own supporters, to English and Scottish Protestants. Uprisings were put down with great savagery in 1649, 1688, and 1798. Ireland became a part of the United Kingdom in 1800.

During the nineteenth century there was famine and starvation in Ireland. Many Irish people fled to foreign lands, such as the United States and Australia. "Fenian" societies were formed in the nineteenth century. They were fighting organizations, struggling for independence. Ireland finally became a Free State in 1922, after the suppression of an uprising in Dublin in 1916. (It became a full republic, independent of the British Empire, in 1948.)

To the dismay of **nationalists**, however, six counties of Ulster, a northern province, remained part of the United Kingdom after 1922. Ulster's inhabitants, most of whom were descended from Protestant immigrants, feared that they would not receive justice as part of Roman Catholic Ireland. Nationalists in the Irish Republican Army (IRA) turned to terrorist attacks in order to fight for a united Ireland.

In 1969 violence broke out once again in Northern Ireland, as nationalists and reformers demanded civil rights for the province's Roman Catholics. British troops were sent in. The British government stated that the soldiers had been sent to protect the Roman Catholic communities from attack by Protestant extremists. However, a bitter struggle soon developed between the British troops and the nationalists. Although the IRA declared a cease-fire in 1972, a breakaway group called

The Grand Hotel in Brighton, England, after a bomb attack by the IRA had killed five. The British Conservative party was meeting for a political conference in the town. The Conservative government is opposed to a united Ireland.

the Provisional IRA (founded in 1969) continued the fight. Attacks on soldiers, police, and politicians became common. Members of the public were often killed in horrific bomb attacks.

Other nationalist groups arose, such as the Irish National Liberation Army (INLA, founded in 1974). Terror organizations such as the Ulster Volunteer Force (UVF, founded as early as 1966) and the Ulster Defense Association (UDA, founded in 1971) were also set up. These groups were made up of Protestant "loyalists," opposed to union with Ireland. They fought their own war against the nationalists with acts of terror carried out against individuals. The Irish troubles have continued into the 1990s. Acts of terror are still committed not only in Ireland, but in England and on the European mainland.

In the headlines 2: Terror in the Middle East

Although the Jews fiercely resisted Roman rule in the first century A.D., they were unsuccessful. Thousands of Jews were sold into slavery and were scattered far and wide across Europe, North Africa, and Asia. They formed their own communities in many countries. Life was uncertain in their adopted countries and Jewish communities were often threatened and destroyed. During the nineteenth century many Jews decided to return to their ancient homeland. Many of the immigrants were Zionists, who believed that the Jewish people were entitled to a permanent home in the region. The region was by then part of the Ottoman (Turkish) Empire and known as Palestine. Most of the people living there were Muslim Arabs. Palestine had been home for these people for many hundreds of years.

During World War I (1914 – 1918), the British fought against Turkey. They encouraged the Palestinian Arabs to revolt against Turkish rule and promised them an independent Arab state when the war was finished. However the British foreign secretary, Lord Balfour, also promised Jewish supporters that a Zionist state would be created in the region. After the war, the international League of Nations asked Britain to govern Palestine in its name.

After World War II (1939 – 1945) the number of Jewish settlers in British Palestine was swollen by those fleeing from Nazi terror in Europe. They demanded a new Jewish state in the region. Some Jewish groups such as *LEHI* ("the Stern gang") and *Irgun Zvai Leumi* ("National Military Organization") used terrorist methods against the British and against Arab and Jewish civilians. *Irgun's* commander-in-chief was Menachem Begin, who from 1977 to 1983 was to serve as prime minister of Israel. One bomb blast at Jerusalem's King David Hotel in 1946 killed 28 British, 41 Palestinian Arabs, and 17 Jews.

The independent state of Israel was founded in 1948, but wars between the new state and its Arab neighbors broke out in 1956, 1967, 1973, and 1982. Israeli troops were successful, and Jews settled on some of the Arab lands their army had occupied.

> We fight and therefore we are.
>
> *Menachem Begin*
> *Commander-in-chief Irgun Zvai Leumi (b.1913)*

Many Palestinian Arabs lived in refugee camps in other countries. They had no state of their own and no way of making their views heard. Like others in such a desperate situation, they turned to terror. Arabs who demanded a Palestinian Arab state and the destruction of Israel founded terrorist organizations such as the Popular Front for the Liberation of Palestine (PFLP). These groups were led by the Palestine Liberation Organization (PLO). Terrorist attacks included the hijacking and bombing of aircraft around the world, kidnapping and hostage-taking, and the murder of tourists. Americans were attacked as well as Jews, because their government had supported Israel.

THE VIOLENT CENTURY

These young Palestinians are under fire from an Israeli military vehicle. Resentment and conflict are common in Palestinian camps such as this one in Gaza.

As the problems of the Palestinian Arabs remained unsolved, the whole region was torn apart by war and terrorism. Lebanon, Israel's northern neighbor, was home to many Palestinian refugees. It collapsed as rival groups attacked each other. Its capital, Beirut, was blasted by the car bombs and rockets of rival terrorists and guerrilla fighters. Americans, Britons, and other foreigners were kidnapped and held hostage. To this day, there has been little progress in solving the problems of the Palestinians.

PAST AND PRESENT

TACTICS, WEAPONS, & VICTIMS

On December 21, 1988 the Pan Am Boeing 747 *Maid of the Seas* was blown apart over Lockerbie, in Scotland. It was flying to New York City, and 270 people were killed. A bomb had been hidden inside a radio-cassette player in the luggage hold.

TACTICS, WEAPONS, & VICTIMS

HOW TERRORISTS ORGANIZE

Terrorist groups often take on military titles, as if they were a regular army. They may form brigades or battalions and give ranks to their members. This helps them to enforce discipline within the groups. Individual members may be treated with great severity and cruelty, or even killed if they disobey orders. The use of military terms may also give the impression to the public that the terrorists are a well-organized force, even if they are not.

When carrying out attacks, terrorists normally form a network of **cells.** These are small groups of people who do not know the names of people in other cells. Only the leader of each cell is in touch with the commanders. This system, developed in the 1950s by the FLN in Algeria, ensures that members who are captured and questioned are unable to give away much useful information.

Many terrorist groups form an armed "wing" of a political party. The party can campaign for the same aim as the terrorists by other legal means. The Social Revolutionary Party, operating in Russia in 1902, existed alongside a "Fighting Organization" that planned assassinations. Provisional Sinn Fein is a political party founded in Northern Ireland to support the aims of the Provisional IRA.

Some terrorist groups have connections in other parts of the world. They seek support from foreign states or come to the aid of foreign terrorist groups, sharing operations or training. Overseas supporters may supply terrorists with funds or weapons. In North America the NORAID organization was founded by Irish Americans to provide aid for the nationalists in Northern Ireland.

WEAPONS OF THE SECRET WAR

Terrorist weapons have changed over the centuries. In ancient Rome or medieval Italy, daggers, swords, and poison were commonly used. On January 31, 1606, an English Roman Catholic called Guy Fawkes was hanged in London. He had been found guilty of planning to blow up the Protestant King James I and his ministers with barrels of gunpowder at the state opening of Parliament on

November 5, 1605. The event is still remembered with bonfires, fireworks, and a children's rhyme:
*Please to remember the Fifth of November
Gunpowder, Treason and Plot.*

Gunpowder was invented in China, and was used in Europe from the fourteenth century. Whether used by armies or by individuals, it was a weapon of terror, making it possible to kill somebody from a distance.

Modern terrorists use all kinds of weapons, from automatic firearms to rocket-launchers and grenades. All of these may kill or cause horrible injuries to large numbers of people in a very short time. The arms may be stolen, purchased from arms dealers, supplied by supporters, or captured during fighting. Even the simplest weapons of the street fighter can be deadly. Fire bombs are made of bottles filled with gasoline and oil or chemicals and then lit by a rag fuse. They burst into flame as they break.

Some of the most savagely cruel weapons injure others more often than the intended victim. For example, bombs sent in letters and parcels may explode at the post office, or bombs placed under parked cars in the street may kill passersby. Sometimes terrorists want the security forces to find a bomb they have placed. When the army or police arrive, a second bomb is exploded by remote control.

THE PUBLIC EYE

Terrorism has always thrived on publicity. Anarchists of the nineteenth century often referred to terrorism as "propaganda by the deed." They meant that each of their acts would give a clear message to the public. The press clearly has a duty to inform people of what is going on. However, in reporting acts of terror, the press helps to create the climate of fear that the terrorists want. Publicity is the terrorists' final weapon.

Today, television carries images of destruction and horror into every home. In 1972 a terrorist group called Black September took 11 Israeli athletes hostage at the Munich Olympic Games. The group demanded the release of 200 Palestinians who were in detention. These

TACTICS, WEAPONS, & VICTIMS

In June 1985 a strange press conference was held at Beirut airport, in Lebanon. American hostages who had been seized during the hijacking of a TWA Boeing 727 said that they were being well treated. They then repeated their captors' demand that prisoners being held in Israel should be freed.

demands were not met. The athletes died and four of the terrorists were killed. Three others were taken prisoner. The horrifying incident was seen by an estimated 800 million television viewers around the world. The sharp increase in terrorism during the 1960s took place at a time when the use of television was becoming worldwide.

THE VICTIMS
The effects of terrorism may continue long after an attack. The relatives of those killed may suffer extreme grief or depression. Some may become obsessed with the desire for revenge or haunted by fear. Children may be orphaned or families left homeless. Those injured may suffer from extreme shock. They may be disabled or blinded and face

serious operations or plastic surgery. If the victims are in a position to inform upon their attackers, they may need a police guard in the hospital. Even hospitals have been targeted by terrorists. Fire fighters, ambulance drivers, and doctors may themselves be attacked.

Terrorism may destroy a community, creating unemployment and poverty. In Lebanon, women and children have been shot in the daily struggle to pass through firing lines in order to get food for the family. In Northern Ireland people have died in revenge killings carried out by extremists on both sides.

The words of this young Palestinian refugee sum up her experience of the violence within her own community. Her right arm was blown off by the grenade attack she describes here.

"I was eighteen. Three of my brothers had died as guerrilla fighters in border raids. Another was in prison here in Jordan. When I did what I did . . . it was a way of avenging my brothers and fighting for my people at the same time. Then I saw that the action I was in had wounded a child. But it was my turn to . . . the man I loved, he yelled at me to throw it, throw the grenade, *throw it*. I loved him more than my own life. But maybe not more than that child's life, I suppose. I couldn't throw it. It exploded. We escaped but he never spoke to me again. I had shamed him in front of his comrades . . . . There are some other women, it seems, who can do it, but I — I am more like the most of us who would like to find a different way. I would like to heal my people, to heal any people. I would like to heal."

> When cruelty is inflicted upon innocent people, it discredits whatever cause.
>
> *Ronald Reagan*
> *U.S. President (1985)*

STATE TERROR

Relatives of the "Disappeared" demand justice after the fall of Argentina's military rulers. They carry photographs of these victims of state terror and demand that the government tries to find out what happened to them.

States have ruled by terror from the earliest times. Kings, emperors, and other rulers have all used mass arrest, seizure of property, torture, and execution in order to crush opposition. The ancient Romans threw Christians to lions as public entertainment. In the Middle Ages in Europe, prisoners rotted in dungeons, had their bodies broken by terrible weapons of torture, or, if they were lucky, met a swift death on the executioner's block. The heads of those executed were displayed on castle walls and bodies were left hanging on public gallows as a terrible warning to others. Rulers in other parts of the world were equally severe. Most ordinary people lived in fear.

> I wish the Roman people had only one neck.
>
> *Caligula, Roman emperor (A.D. 12–41)*

Human rights and freedoms slowly advanced as these rulers were forced to give up their absolute power. However, even when societies became more just and peaceful, many still used slavery, and ruled others according to standards they would not accept themselves. The origins of many modern terrorist problems, from Northern Ireland to Africa, are centuries old.

> Government, even in its best state, is but a necessary evil; in its worst state it is intolerable.
>
> *Thomas Jefferson, U.S. President (1743–1826)*

TYRANTS AND TERROR

During this century new tyrants have used new methods of terror. Perhaps as many as six million people died in the **concentration camps** of Nazi Germany. Most of them were Jews. Transported in cattle trucks, they were systematically murdered in gas ovens. In the Soviet Union, Joseph Stalin was in power from 1929 until his death in 1953. He trusted nobody. He turned ferociously against loyal communists and members of the Red Army, always suspecting they were a threat to his power. In **show trials** he forced them to confess to all kinds of crimes. People were afraid, and the secret police seemed to be everywhere. Between 1937 and 1939 over two thirds of the

STATE TERROR

In 1375 Guillaume de Pommiers was accused of fighting for the king of France when his lands came under the rule of the king of England. He was publicly executed at Bordeaux. In the Middle Ages most monarchs ruled by fear. Enemies were tortured, hanged, burned alive, or beheaded as a lesson to others.

Soviet government's representatives had been arrested or shot. Soviet labor camps were filled with people who showed the slightest resistance to Stalin's policies. Millions perished.

State terrorism continued to occur after World War II. After Cambodia was liberated from Pol Pot, who ruled the country between 1976 and 1979, mass graves were uncovered containing countless skeletons. During military rule in Argentina from 1976 to 1983, about 11,000 people simply disappeared. **Socialists**, democrats,

PAST AND PRESENT

students, journalists, and trade unionists were among those kidnapped by **death squads,** tortured in secret jails and assassinated. Many bodies were dumped into the sea from aircraft. After the fall of the military rulers, demonstrating mothers and grandmothers demanded to be told the fate of those who had disappeared.

In 1960 South African police gunned down 69 peaceful African demonstrators at Sharpeville. They were demonstrating against the "pass laws" introduced by the white (European) minority government. The vast majority of the people in South Africa are African and they had no vote. Under the official policy of *apartheid*, the

For many Africans in South Africa, the apartheid system of government meant that they could be forcibly removed from their homes, as shown here, and resettled in "African" areas, or in faraway "homelands." Penalties for resisting this kind of state violence included beatings, torture, and imprisonment without trial.

races were to be kept separated. Over 80 percent of the land was reserved for whites, and the only Africans allowed to live there were servants. All nonwhites had to carry an official pass in order to travel within their own country. Protesters were terrorized by the police and detained, and many died in custody. By 1990 some reforms were set in motion but Africans still could not vote for the government of their choice.

LIVING UNDER STATE TERROR

The modern state can terrorize people in a number of ways. **Surveillance,** the "bugging" of telephones and houses, makes free conversation impossible. **Censorship** prevents free reporting of news. Secret police and informers prevent meetings and freedom of movement. Opposition leaders may be jailed as terrorists or declared insane and placed in mental institutions, where they are treated with drugs. In Iran, a Death Commission carried out the execution of 2,500 political prisoners in 1988. To outsiders, the state may seem to be running efficiently and legally. The citizens of the state know the truth, but may be scared to admit it publicly.

SPONSORS OF TERRORISM

Some states are criticized as terrorist because they are believed to fund or train terrorist groups working against other countries. In 1986 the United States bombed Libya, in North Africa. Its leader, Muammar Qaddafi, had claimed that he could export terrorism to the heart of America. Libya had already funded various terrorist organizations and provided training for them. Iraq, Iran, and Syria were also accused of sponsoring terrorism.

Opponents of the United States claimed that it, too, had backed terrorists, by funding groups such as the "Contras" during the 1980s. The Contras were fighting the democratically elected socialist government of the Sandanistas in Nicaragua. To American president Ronald Reagan, however, the Contras were freedom fighters. Once again there was the problem of agreeing about who stood for terror and who stood for freedom.

DO DEMOCRACIES USE TERROR?

It is not only **totalitarian** states like Stalin's Soviet Union that use terrorist tactics. Many democratic nations distort the truth "in the public interest." Many have secret services that ignore international laws. Their agents may use espionage, surveillance, sabotage, or even assassination. They aim to destabilize or upset their enemies.

In July 1985 a ship belonging to the ecological group Greenpeace was anchored off New Zealand. The crew of the *Rainbow Warrior* was there to protest against French nuclear tests in the Pacific region. French secret service agents, determined to frighten off the protesters, placed a bomb on board. One crew member was drowned.

In most democracies, laws prevent widespread use of terrorism by the state. However, police or soldiers may take the law into their own hands and commit acts of terror. Many armies from democratic countries use terrorist tactics when fighting overseas. In times of war, atrocities may also occur when officers lose control of individual soldiers or units. In 1967 a United States army patrol at My Lai, in Vietnam, assaulted and murdered 300 innocent villagers, including women and babies. Such war crimes may be the result of soldiers becoming brutalized by war rather than planned campaigns of terror.

> What difference does it make to the dead, the orphans, and the homeless, whether the mad destruction is wrought under the name of totalitarianism or the holy name of liberty and democracy?
>
> *Mohandâs Karamchand Gandhi, (1869–1948)*

THE FIGHT AGAINST TERRORISM

An abandoned car is spotted in Central London. The area is sealed off by police. A bomb disposal officer in protective clothing sends in a robot to check the car for explosives.

ARMY AND POLICE FORCES

Most governments have the money and resources to act against individual groups of terrorists. In the front line are the police, the army, and the emergency services. Between them they can defuse bombs, disperse crowds, put out fires, and transport injured victims to hospitals.

Many countries also have trained special commandos to deal with terrorist emergencies. The Army Delta Force of the United States, the *Grenzchütz* of the former West German state and the British SAS specialize in action against hijackers, bombers, and hostage-takers. The dangers of using such a force are considerable. In Malta in 1985 an Egyptian commando force boarded a hijacked plane in an attempt to rescue the passengers. Tragically, 60 people died in the fighting.

Police forces around the world exchange information about international links between terrorist groups and try to prevent the shipment of arms to terrorists. The American FBI has successfully interrupted and stopped arms shipments, such as antitank cannons intended for Northern Ireland. In the meantime, security forces and airline officials must keep on constant alert at airports. In 1973 airline passengers in the United States had to agree to being searched by security officers for the first time. In that year the authorities seized 2,000 guns and nearly 3,500 lb (1,600 kg) of explosives. Over 3,000 people were arrested at American airports.

USING THE LAW

A government may use special laws to silence groups it considers to be terrorist. In Britain, for example, it is illegal to show past or present television interviews with members of the IRA or Sinn Fein (although the words of the interview may be spoken by an actor). But because censorship laws stop people from saying what they think, they are often unpopular with the public.

If countries are faced by a long-term problem of political terrorism, they may allow the security forces to detain people without trial for long periods. Such laws may be effective, but they restrict people's freedom.

THE FIGHT AGAINST TERRORISM

When members of the Red Brigades went on trial in Italy, they were caged in the courtroom and heavily guarded in order to prevent rescue attempts.

Prisoners and detainees can also often become more damaging behind bars than when free. They may become symbols of resistance to government. The anarchist Adolf Fischer, one of those wrongly convicted of the Chicago bombing in 1886, said before his execution: "This is the happiest day of my life!" He knew that he and his fellows would be seen as heroes by revolutionaries elsewhere, and that this would help them in their struggle.

> We must try to find ways to starve the terrorist and hijacker of the oxygen of publicity on which they depend.
>
> *Margaret Thatcher,*
> *former British prime minister (1985)*

QUESTIONS OF RIGHT AND WRONG

Is nonviolence the alternative to terrorism? In 1930 Gandhi called on Indians to break the law that allowed only the government to produce salt. He led an unarmed march to Dandi to collect salt from the sea.

The use of violence and terror raises many questions about what we believe. Some people reject all use of violence and refuse to take human life. Religious groups such as the Society of Friends (or Quakers) regard all warfare as evil. The Jains of India refuse to take life and oppose warfare. Many who have no religious faith share these beliefs.

AGAINST ALL VIOLENCE

Can society be changed or injustice cured by nonviolent action? The *Swaraj* movement opposed British rule in India during the 1920s and 1930s. Instead of turning to terror, its leader, Mohandâs Karamchand Gandhi, turned to nonviolent **civil disobedience.** He led protest marches and hunger strikes and refused to pay taxes. Gandhi believed that by this moral example India would become free. India did become independent in 1947, but tragically Gandhi was assassinated the following year by a right-wing Hindu extremist.

Gandhi's campaign had been successful, but it had failed to prevent widespread bloodshed. Some people wondered whether the campaign would have been as successful if his enemy had been a totalitarian state such as Nazi Germany. However, many believed that Gandhi was indeed *"Mahatma,"* a "Great Soul." Gandhi's ideas of nonviolent political action influenced many other protest movements, such as the British "Campaign for Nuclear Disarmament" (CND) which began its protests against nuclear weapons in the 1950s.

RELIGIOUS VIEWS OF TERROR

Some Christians believe that warfare is acceptable in order to oppose injustice. In the Middle Ages, Christians and Muslims fought "holy" wars against each other. Many religions still believe in the idea of holy wars. In recent years, Sikh militants in the Golden Temple in Amritsar have carried automatic weapons and Iranian Shiite Muslims have trained to use machine guns in defense of their faith. Conflict between Protestant and Roman Catholic Christians has played a part in the Northern Ireland troubles.

A fierce argument breaks out between Sikhs at Amritsar in India. Their holiest shrine, the Golden Temple in Amritsar, became the site of murder and army assault during the 1980s. Throughout history, religious beliefs have set off violence and terrorism.

Some Christians today will support wars, but only those that are carried out by regular armies. Others have advocated the use of violence by guerrillas fighting racist or terrorist governments, or those that oppress the poor. Such ideas have been put forward by priests working in Central and South America. Many of them have been terrorized by government death squads. In El Salvador, even the Archbishop, Oscar Romero, was gunned down in 1980.

MORAL ISSUES

The ancient Roman politician Cicero once wrote that the killing of a tyrant was "the finest of all glorious deeds." Some people have suggested that single acts of violence are more acceptable than full-scale wars. If Adolf Hitler had been assassinated before World War II, perhaps the lives

QUESTIONS OF RIGHT AND WRONG

of millions of soldiers and victims might have been saved. Assassins risk only their own lives.

Most sane human beings cannot commit an atrocity or kill another human being easily. They experience guilt or horror. Many assassins have turned away from the terrible deed at the last moment. In 1905 the assassin of the Russian Grand Duke Sergei refused to kill children traveling in the same carriage as the intended victim. Two days later, however, he killed the grand duke when he was traveling alone.

Terrorist groups try to overcome their human feelings by training their members to see people as enemies rather than as individuals. Armies train their soldiers in much the same way. In the end though, human beings have to decide the moral questions for themselves. They have to decide whether all violence is wrong or whether only certain kinds of violence are wrong.

UN forces control a checkpoint on the Golan Heights, between Syria and territory occupied by Israel. The United Nations can attack the problem of terrorism in two ways. It can police areas of trouble. More importantly, it can encourage political solutions and thus remove the injustice that is at the root of terrorist violence.

THE FUTURE?

At the end of the twentieth century, the world is still divided into regions of great poverty and great wealth. There is injustice and strife. There are still governments that terrorize their own citizens and politicians who turn to war instead of discussion in order to settle their differences.

It seems likely that terrorism will continue to thrive in the future. It will be met on the streets with new weapons. The use of computers and electronic surveillance in the fight against terrorism will become more widespread.

However, until the opponents of terrorism try to understand the problem and its root causes, they cannot win. And until terrorists act with humanity toward their fellow human beings, they cannot win either.

On November 8, 1793 a French woman called Jeanne Manon Phlipon, wife of the reformer Jean-Marie Roland de la Platière, was sent to the guillotine. She had condemned the Reign of Terror. On her way to the guillotine, Madame Roland is said to have cried "Oh Liberty! What crimes are committed in thy name!"

KEY DATES

B.C. 44
Political murder: Assassination of Julius Caesar by republican conspirators in Rome.

A.D. 1192
Religious murder: Conrad of Montferrat, Christian king of Jerusalem, fatally stabbed by *hashshashin*, a Muslim group, active in Persia and Syria.

1605
Explosives as a weapon of terror: "The Gunpowder Plot" was a plan to blow up the English king and parliament. Gunpowder intended for the attack is discovered in a nearby cellar.

1798
First recorded use of the word "terrorism": An official French dictionary defines it as *"système, régime de terreur"* or "system of government by terror."

1808
Introduction of the word "guerrilla": Meaning "small war," used to describe the hit-and-run tactics used by the Spanish and Portuguese against the occupying French forces in the Peninsular War.

1881–1901
Challenging the old order: New political ideas lead some to adopt violent ways of changing society. Wave of bomb attacks and assassinations of national rulers in Europe and the United States.

1914
Consequences of a political murder: Assassination of the archduke of Austria by a Serbian nationalist sets in motion a chain of events leading directly to the outbreak of World War I.

1936
Weapons of state terror: Stalin uses informers and secret police to send thousands of Soviet party representatives to imprisonment and execution.

1954
Guerrilla warfare: The National Liberation Front begins a guerrilla campaign in the battle for Algeria's independence. Other freedom fighters adopt similar tactics.

1972
International terrorism: Seven "Black September" Palestinian terrorists capture 11 Israeli athletes at Munich Olympic Games, killing two, and holding the others hostage. Incident ends in shootout at airport and the death of all hostages and four terrorists.

1985
Long-term campaigns: The Provisional IRA marks 25 years of its terrorist campaign by bombing a hotel in Brighton, England, where members of the Conservative party were staying during their annual party conference.

1986
State support of terrorism: United States bombs Libya for supporting terrorism.

GLOSSARY

anarchism: A political theory that blames state control for misery and poverty. Anarchists believe that society functions best if groups and individuals are left to work together at a local level. Some anarchists reject the use of violence. Others support the use of terror.

assassin: 1) Someone who murders for a reward or for a belief. 2) Somebody who murders a famous person.

cell: A self-contained unit within a revolutionary group that answers only to central command.

censorship: The suppression of news, books or plays by an army or government because of security or for political, religious, or moral reasons.

civil disobedience: Refusing to obey laws or pay taxes for political reasons.

colony: 1) A settlement of people in a new land. 2) A land that is governed by an overseas power. A large number of former colonies won their independence in the 1950s and 1960s. For some, such as Angola and Mozambique, colonial rule led to long and bitter wars.

communism: A social system based on common ownership. In some countries this took the form of total state control of the production of goods. Some communists supported the use of terror in the fight against capitalism, but Karl Marx (1818 – 1883) and his supporters rejected terrorism. They believed that capitalism would fail and that the masses would then seize power.

concentration camp: Originally, a camp where civilians were imprisoned during war, as used by the British during the Anglo-Boer War in South Africa. Later, the word was used to describe the centers for murder and forced labor set up by the Nazis in Europe.

death squads: Gangs who kidnap and murder their opponents, often with the approval of a terrorist state.

fascism: A social theory tried in Italy between 1922 and 1943. The state, anticommunist and extremely nationalist, governed by terror. It sought total control and allowed no opposition. People trying to revive fascism today are called "neofascists."

guerrilla: An irregular fighter who attacks an army — from the Spanish word for "little war."

heresy: A religious belief which is said to run against the teachings of that particular religion. Those holding such beliefs are called heretics.

GLOSSARY

hijacking: To steal goods in transit or to seize and divert a vehicle, holding any passengers hostage. Terrorists have hijacked planes, ships, and trains. The word was first used in the United States in the 1920s. Hijacking a plane is sometimes called skyjacking.

hostage-taking: Holding someone as protection against attack or as a bargaining counter; using someone as a "human shield."

nationalist: 1) Someone who wishes independence for his or her country. 2) Someone who supports his or her nation above all others.

neofascist: See fascism.

propaganda: Information or lies spread in order to help a particular group or theory or to harm a rival.

racist: Emphasizing differences or encouraging hatred among races or ethnic groups.

sabotage: Damage or destruction to factories, tools, communications, or power installations. The word may have its origin in a French railway strike of 1910. *Sabots* (literally, "wooden shoes") fixed the railway tracks to the ties. Angry strikers pulled out these *sabots* so that trains could not run.

show trial: A trial in which the defendant is publicly forced to declare his or her guilt, regardless of the evidence. This is often part of the propaganda devised by the state to caution the population.

socialism: Any social system based on common ownership. The term can be used to describe the beliefs of communists or of democrats who support a certain amount of public ownership within a capitalist state.

state terrorism: Use by a government of terrorizing methods such as violent attack, kidnapping, and murder.

surveillance: A watch kept over persons, for example by a government over its citizens or by police over terrorists or other criminals. Surveillance may include following a suspect, watching all movements, listening in to private telephone or radio conversations, or opening mail.

terrorism: The extreme use of violence and crimes against the person in order to achieve a political or other social aim. The term was first used to describe the actions of a state against its citizens. Later it was used to describe also the actions of individuals against the state or against innocent people. Its use suggests criticism of those described as "terrorists."

totalitarian: A government that allows no opposition, either from political parties or individuals.

urban guerrilla: Somebody taking up arms to fight in the city rather than open countryside. The term is often used by city terrorists to describe themselves.

INDEX

Africa 18, 19, 23, 32, 34, 35
anarchism 13, 14, 15, 28, 39
Argentina 31, 33
arson 7, 19
assassination 10, 14, 15, 17, 34, 36, 42, 43
Austria 15, 17

Baader-Meinhof group 20
Barcelona bombing 15
Bologna bombing 20
bombs 5, 7, 14, 15, 19, 23, 24, 25, 26, 28, 36, 37, 38
Britain 17, 18, 20, 21, 23, 24, 38, 41

Chicago bombing 14, 15, 39
Christianity 11, 31, 41, 42
commandos 38
communism 13, 17, 32

death squads 34, 42

Egypt 10, 38
Ethniki Organosis Kyprion Agoniston (EOKA) 19
Euzkadi ta Askatasuna (ETA) 19
executions 13, 32, 33, 35, 39

fascism 20
Fawkes, Guy 27
France 11, 13, 14, 15, 17, 18, 19, 20, 33, 36
freedom fighters 4, 7, 8, 35
French Revolution 11, 12, 13, 44
Front de Liberation National (FLN) 18, 19, 27

Germany 16, 17, 20, 32, 38
Greece 10, 20
guerrillas 8, 18, 21, 25, 30, 42

hashshashin 10
hijacking 7, 24, 29, 39
hostage-taking 7, 24

India 40, 41, 42
Iran 10, 35, 41
Ireland 21, 22, 27, 30, 32, 38, 41
Irgun Zvai Leumi (National Military Organization) 24
Irish Republican Army (IRA) 5, 21, 22, 27, 38
Israel 24, 25, 28, 29
Italy 14, 15, 20, 39

Jews 10, 16, 17, 23, 24, 32

kidnapping 19, 20, 24, 25
King David's Hotel bombing 24

Lebanon 25, 29, 30
Libya 35
Lockerbie disaster 26

Malta hijack 38
Munich Olympics massacre 28
murder 10, 17, 19, 20, 24, 42
Muslims 10, 11, 23, 41
My Lai massacre 36

Nazis (National Socialist Party) 16, 17, 18, 20, 24, 32, 41
Nicaragua 4, 35

Palestine 23, 24, 25, 28, 30
People's Will (*Narodnaya Volya*) 13
police 15, 19, 23, 28, 30, 35, 36, 37, 38
Pol Pot 33
Provisional Sinn Fein 27, 38
publicity 10, 28, 39

Rainbow Warrior bombing 36
Red Army (*Sekigun*) of Japan 20
Red Brigades 20, 39
revolution 11, 13, 20
robbery 19, 20
Rome 10, 23, 27, 31
Russia 13, 17, 20, 27, 43

Scotland 18, 26
separatism 18, 19
slavery 23, 32
Social Revolutionary Party 27
Soviet Union 32, 33, 36
Spain 15, 18
state terrorism 7, 11, 17, 31, 32, 33, 34, 35, 36
Stern Gang 24
Syria 10, 35, 43

Ulster Defense Association (UDA) 23
Ulster Volunteer Force (UVF) 23
United Nations (UN) 7, 8, 43
United States of America 4, 15, 20, 21, 27, 30, 35, 36, 38

weapons 5, 7, 19, 25, 26, 28, 44